After the Wedding...

A **DIVORCE LAWYER'S** TOP 25 TIPS TO **KEEP YOU MARRIED**

BONNIE ROBERTSON, ESQ.

After the Wedding...

© 2023 Bonnie Robertson, Esq.

ISBN 979-8-35092-845-7

eBook ISBN 979-8-35092-846-4

CONTENTS

PROLOGUE

For more than two decades, I have had a front-row seat to other people's marital problems. I am the person with whom they share their deepest regrets, their resentments, their secrets. By the time a person is consulting with me, their marriage is generally all but over. Arkansas, where I am licensed to practice law, is still one of the states that requires a party to a divorce to establish that their spouse is at "fault" for the demise of the marriage. It's an archaic requirement, generally based on the premise that marriage is sacred, and the government should not be allowed to easily wreck it.

From a practical standpoint, requiring a person to establish fault requires attorneys to delve into, formulate, and ultimately prove that our client has been sufficiently wronged to be granted a divorce.

Thus, in every one of the hundreds and hundreds of divorces I litigate, I have a detailed and intimate view into the things that ruin a marriage.

Throughout this book, please remember the issues discussed assume that the relationship does not include what I call "the 3 Big As." Those are Addiction, Adultery, and Abuse. When one or more of these problems exists in a marriage, the game changes, and these tips are not useful. With these tips, I do not purport to address resolution of the 3 Big As. If your marriage includes a Big A, I hope you are able to get the help, healing, and if necessary, the legal dissolution you need.

These tips are not in order of importance or profundity. They are meant to be read then reread, as necessary. The issues or opportunities they represent will come at different times for different couples. Some will provide helpful reminders of things you can do to improve or maintain your healthy marital relationship.

I want to mention and thank my mom for her never-ending assistance and unwavering support throughout my life—including in finalizing this book. I am also grateful to Traci Berry, whose appreciation for this work inspired me to finally put these tips to a higher use than a social media project. And of course, I want to thank my husband, Brian, for our beautiful marriage and our beautiful children we have created, developed, and enjoyed together for all of these years.

#1: IF YOU WOULDN'T RUN A BUSINESS WITH THIS PERSON, DON'T MARRY THEM.

Consider which characteristics and virtues are vital to establishing, building, and maintaining a successful business: ambition, integrity, self-discipline, commitment, ingenuity, maturity, organizational skills, tenacity, and perhaps most important—strong work ethic.

These same desirable characteristics apply to raising children, helping care for the house, yard, pets. They apply to friendships and neighborhood relationships, and they apply to the general culture of your marriage.

When you begin seriously dating this person, consider how they run the business side of their life. Do they pay their bills on time? Do they go to work every day, or do they miss a lot of work? Do they change jobs often? If so, why? Are their housekeeping skills adequate, or is their space so sloppy you are uncomfortable being there? Are they saving money, or do they spend everything they earn? It is so important to assess whether this person will be a good business-of-marriage partner.

#2: YOU KNOW WHAT'S SEXY, FUN, AND GIVES BACK IN SPADES? A SPOUSE WHO HAS THEIR OWN SH*T GOING ON.

You should encourage and support your spouse's hobbies, interests, career. You should be glad they have a group of friends and family they can rely on and hang out with.

You don't have to be involved in every pursuit. The happiest marriages I observe have two people who do not resent each other's separate endeavors.

If you tend to get nervous or insecure about not being with them at all times, that's not love, that's not devotion. That's your baggage, and your spouse shouldn't have to carry it.

#3: YOU'RE MARRIED, NOT DEAD.

Unless you were literally the only boyfriend/girlfriend each other ever had (also its own recipe for a difficult marriage—but not always!), there is history. There are exes. And unless you isolate yourself in the house, you'll occasionally find other people interesting and attractive. That's normal.

Where you must take great care is in your interactions with others. It really is as simple as your conversation.

Make a rule that you will never have a conversation (in-person or online) with one of these people that you wouldn't have if your spouse were sitting right there or also reading the messages. Govern yourself and your vibe.

If you feel tempted, it may be because things are a little dull or tumultuous at home. "Tend to your own grass, don't go to another lawn." Conversations can be a slippery slope, so don't even sit on that slide. Protect your marriage and honor your spouse, simply through the words you never speak.

#4: LEAN IN CLOSE, Y'ALL.

Have SEX O.F.T.E.N. (And not just for the reasons you might think.)

Consider what frequent sex requires: time out from all else, focus on each other, creativity, spontaneity, keeping yourself healthy, giving your spouse what only you can (should) give. Those items are a recipe for success even outside the realm of physical contact.

So apply them, don't get lazy, and you will find yourself attracted to your spouse, even decades into the marriage.

When you hit dry spells, And you WILL, let it bother you. Let it worry you. Let it become a problem you feel compelled to solve. Don't ignore it. Fix it.

#5 WHAT ARE THE OTHER LONG-MARRIED PEOPLE THINKING?

This section comes from a few very special and savvy married couples. And I couldn't have been more delighted by their input. I know these gems will utterly inspire you as well.

FROM MARK & TERRI, married 35 years:

Your actions are much more powerful than your words. Sometimes it's just about little things like taking the trash out or fixing your spouse a sandwich.

And saying 'please, thank you' or just 'I love you' is VERY important. Don't take them for granted. Keep your promises.

Priorities change as the clock ticks.

For us – it is

1. God

2. Family

3. Work

4. Etc.

FROM GRADY & DAVE, together for 21 years:

Everyone has a past. I learned a long time ago that having a relationship with anyone (gay, straight, platonic or sexual) means having to understand that you need to have a patient and respectful relationship with their past. It is how they have handled their past that shapes their future and those who are in it.

If you love your partner, love them. This means understanding their history, their quirks and faults.

Love your partner the way you want to be loved by them.

Avoid ultimatums unless you are 100% prepared to follow through with either option.

Love is love.

FROM MARK & KIM, married 26 years:

Kim and I are believers in Jesus Christ and try to model His teaching in life and our marriage.

Love is a daily decision. We don't always "like" each other, but we have committed to "love" each other biblically. Our love for one another isn't based on feelings because they are inconsistent and fleeting – twenty six years of marriage has taught us that.

The love we share, while not perfect, is intentional and unconditional.

FROM GINA & BRAD, married 30 years:

Change in marriage is inevitable. Not only jobs, finances , or neighborhoods, but also personalities, priorities, once firmly-held beliefs about the world, and even hopes and dreams.

It takes work and good communication to take your spouse along.

Nostalgia is a natural human emotion. And yet being forever content with a spouse requires finding ways to be happy with different versions of that person. Remember, though, all work and no play DOES make one dull. It's ok, even recommended, to revisit those places and things that brought you joy years ago. But don't linger there. Keep rediscovering.

#6: WHAT ARE THE DIVORCED PEOPLE THINKING?

This tip comes from people who are divorced.
The 1st is from one of my former divorce clients;
the 2nd is from my mom, who was married to my dad for 29 years.

My question to them was: "looking back at your marriage (that ended in divorce), what would YOU have done differently if you had known to do it differently?"

From my client, C.M.:

- constant self-assessment in terms of how I can be a better partner.

- accepting accountability for my part, from house chores to disputes.

- respecting (my spouse) as an equal and acknowledging the value they bring to the relationship.

- being open and honest with my true feelings, even if it's embarrassing.

- listening

- working to solve small issues before they become big ones.

- remembering that I serve more than just myself.

From my mom:

I was only 16 years old when I got married. Although mature for my age, I was not even close to developing the tools to be married. I always thought that yelling, having temper tantrums, and trying to loudly insist on what I wanted was the only way to handle problems. It never occurred to me to simply ask if we could talk through an issue. It never occurred to me to actually sit down and try to listen to each other. So problems really never got solved. They got pushed down the road, festered, and grew bigger.

(Side note: From my point of view as their kid, they weren't really what I would call a "happy couple." But they functioned, raised four kids, waited for me-the youngest – to turn 18 before divorcing. The virtue of that decision is debatable, of course. But one thing they always did right was leave us kids out of their conflicts. No matter what was going on between them, they spoke love and respect for each other to us kids – always. They always came together, sat together, enjoyed their children for holidays and our school events, sports games. We never had to choose between them. Never. And most delightfully, they remained literally best friends until my dad passed away in 2018. I am so grateful to them for showing us love in that way. It informed how I behaved in my own blended family, and it informs how I counsel my clients. I love you, Mom.)

#7: LET'S TALK ABOUT ROTTEN MARRIAGE SEEDS THAT WILL BEAR ROTTEN FRUIT. SO DON'T PLANT THESE SEEDS.

A. Threatening the "D" word. Don't even say it. Enter your marriage and maintain your years with the philosophy that divorce is simply not an option. Easier said than done, for sure. But if you are both taking care of business most of the time, this isn't as difficult as it might seem.

Several of my clients reported that the threat of divorce or one of them leaving was a common "tactic" in their arguments. I think we as a society have learned to throw this around, because it is just so common. But even allowing that to come out of your mouth is very damaging to the relationship—especially if you don't mean it. Eventually, it becomes an easy subject, and chances are, you are wearing your spouse down with this threat. At some point, the ease of thinking about it makes it a real option.

B. Moving out or demanding your spouse move out. Just don't. Once you do, it's going to be very difficult (not impossible) to turn that train around.

Of course, getting some physical distance or a short period of time might be a good thing—depending on the situation. But as tempting as it may be, do not use your leaving as a way to hurt your spouse's feelings or to attempt to manipulate your spouse. Leaving should be a purposeful, necessary tool to work toward resolution, not to punish. One of the fundamentals of any relationship is kindness. You would not likely use physical distance as a way to punish or make your friend feel worse. Why would you do that to your spouse?

C. Thinking that (temporarily) disliking your spouse means the marriage is doomed. Again, if you meant "forever" at your wedding, you'll go through awful, tumultuous, very unpleasant marital seasons lasting days, weeks, months, maybe years. Keep working. It's worth it.

#8: THE HILL YOU DIE ON BETTER HAVE A BEAUTIFUL VIEW.

Pick your battles. No, really. Pick them, and fight them.

But make sure what you are fighting for is truly important enough to cause all this trouble and stress.

Then do the work of communicating, compromising, listening, and trying to understand your spouse's point of view.

Will this be so important in a year? Two years? In the grand scheme of your life?

You don't always have to win. You don't always have to die on that hill. Sometimes, just march right back down, let it go, and live to fight another day.

#9: THE PERSON YOU MARRIED— WHO WILL NOW HELP RAISE YOUR CHILDREN FROM A PREVIOUS RELATIONSHIP—NEEDS YOUR FIERCE PROTECTION.

Most of the time, they love you first, then they grow to love your children. Their role among you, your kids, and the kids' other parent will be one of the most difficult roles they ever take on.

Defend them.

Allow them space to develop their special relationship with your kids.

Be realistic and clear in what you need from them. Be compassionate and supportive.

And remember, if you do it right, your marriage will long outlast the childhoods and the challenges of navigating the blended family dynamic. And when all of that is behind you, it's oh-so-awesome to still have each other.

(The blended family subject really deserves its own volume of tips. But I want to add a couple onto this list, just to give homage to the importance of being mindful, if this is your situation.)

#10: IT'S 3 TIMES THE WORK, MISERY, WONDER, REWARD, TEARS, JOY, FRUSTRATION, INSECURITY, AND HAPPINESS WITH THE 2ND SPOUSE.

I'm addressing the "blended family." The "step-parent factor." This subject is very complex, I was reluctant to even touch on it. But here goes:

As the 2nd spouse/step-parent, do not marry into this if you cannot encourage, facilitate, even insist upon healing and PEACE with the other parent. It doesn't have to be friendship or even positive feelings toward the 1st spouse/parent, although that is ideal and much more healthy for your own soul.

Conflict with the former spouse/other parent is one of most common stressors I observe in my representation, and my clients often come to me for their second divorces, within a couple of years. Therefore, I try to counsel my client and their current spouse about not letting the stress seep too far in between them.

Here's just one tidbit-oversimplified, under-developed example: Mostly stay out of the parenting issues between your spouse and the former spouse.

Let them handle their troubles, even if you would handle it differently.

You're a player on their team, not their coach. (So much more to say on this, but not here.)

#11: SHARE MONEY.

If this tip triggered indignance, still read to the end.

Through my divorce practice, I've developed this non-scientific theory that couples who do not share money tend to lack depth in other areas of their relationship.

(I do acknowledge that tons of marriages survive even though the couple have separate accounts and pay separate bills, etc.)

But consider the marital skills we must develop in order to successfully share money, all of which are vital to a HAPPY marriage: cooperation, compromise, transparency, commitment to the financial success of the partnership, and mutual respect.

So you two have philosophical differences related to money? Well, guess what, raising kids will be no different. And I definitely would not advise splitting them so you each get to raise one as you please.

Instead of immediately deciding to separate funds so you can save or spend as you please, consider doing the hard, uncomfortable work of combining your money. Find ways to compromise and cooperate in running this business of marriage together.

#12: DON'T HURT YOUR SPOUSE.

Well, duh. Right? This is a deeper, much more challenging concept after first blush.

(And again, I'm not attempting to tackle the 3 big As.)

Does your spouse complain that you work too much? You drink too much? You spend too much money? That they need more help around the house, yard, with the kids?

Maybe you disagree, you don't see these problems, you feel justified in continuing whatever behavior is hurting your spouse, and your spouse needs to simply back off, lighten up, get over it, etc.

Here's the reality: continued "hurts" are the reason only about 50% of marriages survive. Not adultery, not some major injury or insult.

It's the slow, subtle, poisonous creep of The Hurts—those hurtful behaviors people indignantly persist in and insist on, while assuming their spouse will eventually be OK.

Therefore, you'll need to contemplate cost vs. benefit of your choices, compromise where you possibly can. Your marriage likely and literally depends on it.

#13: BRACE YOURSELVES, THIS IS A HARD ONE: THE PROBLEMS IN YOUR MARRIAGE ARE <u>YOUR</u> FAULT.

Stay with me.

Imagine if you BOTH always tried to find your own contribution to the difficult issues in your relationship. Imagine if the discussions of those issues started with both of you identifying your own fears, weaknesses, "baggage" that created part of the problem, and what you, yourself, could do better as it relates to the problem.

I can't think of many marital problems that didn't take 2 married people to create.

Ugh. Makes your brain hurt. It's so counterintuitive. "What if they can't see their fault in the problem? I need to make sure they know what they've done wrong."

Well, what if you put all of that aside, sincerely and honestly discuss what YOU will work on improving, and without strings attached or expectation of the same in return? Chances are, your spouse will follow suit. Try it next time.

#14: IF YOU THINK SOMETHING NICE, SAY SOMETHING NICE.

Who doesn't love hearing they look good in a pair of jeans, or that their spouse is proud of how hard they worked on a project, or any small, yet sincere compliment?

Keep making those proverbial deposits into your marriage "account". Don't ever assume your spouse knows that you still notice.

#15: GO TO BED MAD.

I understand the philosophy of the old adage that states the opposite.

But sometimes a night's sleep is exactly what you both need when you're dealing with something painful and troublesome.

The important point is to make sure you come BACK to the issue in order to continue talking, crying, working, even if it's a new day and you would really just prefer to forget about it.

Remember that problems don't usually disappear, they linger and hover, and fester. Keep working.

#16: DO THINGS TOGETHER THAT MAKE YOU LAUGH.

Chances are, you laughed together in the early years. Don't lose that. Find time to have fun and let go together.

Every year, but especially during the years of career development and raising young children, make a BIG deal of anniversaries and birthdays-sometimes those will be the only 3 times in that year you'll stop to enjoy and honor each other.

#17: YES. THEY WOULD ALSO LIKE A CUP OF COFFEE.

Be thoughtful, intentional, and kind, for no particular reason or occasion.

One thing I tend to observe when I'm around couples is whether they are truly kind to each other.

I don't mean displays of affection or sappy social media posts. We all know those can be deceiving.

But kindness that stems from true respect and regard for their partner's comfort and happiness. And hopefully when we see that in public, that healthy culture exists in the privacy of their home.

#18: YOU KNOW THAT ATTRIBUTE OF THEIRS THAT ANNOYS YOU?

(THEIR "OCD", THEIR PENCHANT FOR DRAMA, THEIR INABILITY TO RELAX, THEIR INAPPROPRIATE HUMOR, ETC.)

Think hard. Chances are, that same attribute was part of what attracted you to them in the beginning (Their tenacity, their passion, their ambition, their sense of humor).

Remember there are 2 sides to coins, and you cannot expect them to shut off who they are until or unless it's useful or fun for you. (This of course doesn't include harmful or selfish behavior that serves no positive purpose).

P.S. My momma gets credit for helping me realize this one.

P.P.S. When I asked Brian Robertson to give me examples of things that annoy him but that he also appreciates, I finally had to tell him I had enough examples. 😣

#19: TRAVEL TOGETHER.

Even if it's a "staycation" in town. Regularly go away together from your day-to-day surroundings, your kids, your home. It's truly the best way to quiet your minds and remind yourselves why you like each other.

Can't afford it, you say? No time, you say?

Well, do you find a way to afford the gym because you value your health and fitness? Do you find a way to make time for your favorite sports or streaming channel because you value the entertainment and relaxation they provide? Could you do without the fancy drive-through coffee for a month or two and save that money? Do you have a hobby that costs money?

If so, then you can find money and time to maintain your marriage—because you value it.

#20: YOU WILL GET BORED.

If this is forever, it will get so boring at times. This may last days, weeks, even months.

You will be uncomfortable. You might even mistake boredom for some serious problem or something you need to change. But sit in it. Recognize it for what it is-a natural thing that happens in all aspects of our lives.

Then communicate with your spouse. Do a welfare check on the relationship. If things are otherwise as they should be, then suck it up, do something new and exciting with your spouse.

Then do another new and exciting thing, and another, and this will pass.

#21: YOUR CHILDREN COME SECOND TO YOUR MARRIAGE.

Yes. That's what I said.

In order to keep your children's parents (that's you) HAPPILY married, the children should be in your marital orbit, not in the center. Someday, they will thank you.

What I mean is this: if parenthood, kids' activities, etc. is your reason for low intimacy, never traveling together, never focusing on each other, the kids are too far in the center of the family. It will eventually kill your marriage. I litigated countless divorces in which the couple simply did not relate or even "know" each other after the kids left home. They had focused so much on the children, they forgot to maintain their own relationship.

#22: ARGUE.

Get mad, get annoyed. Never arguing means you aren't interested enough. It means you aren't plugged in to the health of your relationship.

As years pass, arguments should become more rare. But pay attention. The work is never done.

Establish any additional rules you and your spouse need to set, in order to have healthy arguments.

RULE: NEVER, and I mean never, call each other names during arguments. Never throw personal insults.

#23: DO NOT TREAT YOUR SPOUSE WITH LESS KINDNESS THAN YOU TREAT YOUR CLOSE FRIENDS.

Not in the way you speak to them, listen to them, consider them, support them, accept them, and forgive them.

As a divorce lawyer, I can say this is one of the most consequential mistakes I observe.

It seems like a simple concept, but putting this into practice can be a challenge, especially if you have poor examples of marriage and romantic relationships throughout your life.

#24: YOU BOTH SHOULD HAVE INTERESTS AND PASSIONS IN COMMON AND IN WHICH THE OTHER HAS ZERO INTEREST.

And stay out of it. In those pursuits, let them be and do without you. You'll both grow so much better together if you are also allowed to love and serve your separate self from time to time.

#25: USE THIS BOOK AS YOUR MARRIAGE JOURNAL.

The most enduring and important gift Brian and I received at our wedding was our marriage journals.

Throughout the year, but at a minimum when we take our anniversary trip, we take the journals with us and make an entry in the other's journal. The entries are not just sweet words. Instead, we sometimes address a tough time we had that year or a challenge we are currently working on.

As the years pass, it's awesome to reread what we've written to each other from Year One to the present. After so many years, reading and rereading the entries brings laughter, tears, reminiscence, and beautiful realization how much we've grown.

Use the following pages as your marriage journal. Be intentional in continually breathing life and passion into your relationship. The grass will not grow unless you tend to it, and I hope this book provides you some of the water.